W9-AFE-200

George Washington

written and illustrated by
Rod Espinosa

red
wagon

visit us at
www.abdopublishing.com

Published by Red Wagon, a division of the ABDO Publishing Group, 8000 West 78th Street, Edina, Minnesota 55439. Copyright © 2008 by Abdo Consulting Group, Inc. International copyrights reserved in all countries. All rights reserved. No part of this book may be reproduced in any form without written permission from the publisher. Graphic Planet™ is a trademark and logo of Red Wagon.

Printed in the United States.

Written and illustrated by Rod Espinosa
Colored and lettered by Rod Espinosa
Edited by Stephanie Hedlund
Interior layout and design by Antarctic Press
Cover art by Rod Espinosa
Cover design by Neil Klinepier

Library of Congress Cataloging-in-Publication Data

Espinosa, Rod.
    George Washington / written and illustrated by Rod Espinosa.
    p. cm. -- (Bio-graphics)
    Includes index.
    ISBN 978-1-60270-067-3
    1. Washington, George, 1732-1799--Juvenile literature. 2. Presidents--United States--Biography --Juvenile literature. 3. Graphic novels. I. Title.

E312.66.E77 2008
973.4'1092--dc22
[B]   2007004349

TABLE of CONTENTS

Timeline

1732 - On February 22, George Washington was born to Augustine and Mary Washington.

1748 - Washington became a surveyor.

1754 to 1758 - Washington fought as a commissioned officer in the French and Indian War.

1759 - Washington married Martha Dandridge Custis.

1774 - Washington attended the First Continental Congress as the delegate from Virginia and was named the Commander in Chief of the Continental Forces.

1776 - Washington led the attack on Trenton.

1777 to 1778 - Washington and his troops camped at Valley Forge.

1781 - Cornwallis surrendered to Washington at Yorktown; the Revolutionary War ended.

1789 - Washington was inaugurated the first President of the United States.

1797 - Washington completed his second term as president and refused a third term; he returned to Mount Vernon.

1799 - Washington died on December 14 at Mount Vernon at the age of 67.

George Washington was an American patriot, a soldier, and a general. He also helped found the United States of America, and then he became its first president. He lived a life full of greatness and purpose.

To tell this story we must start at the beginning...

Chapter 1 Growing Up

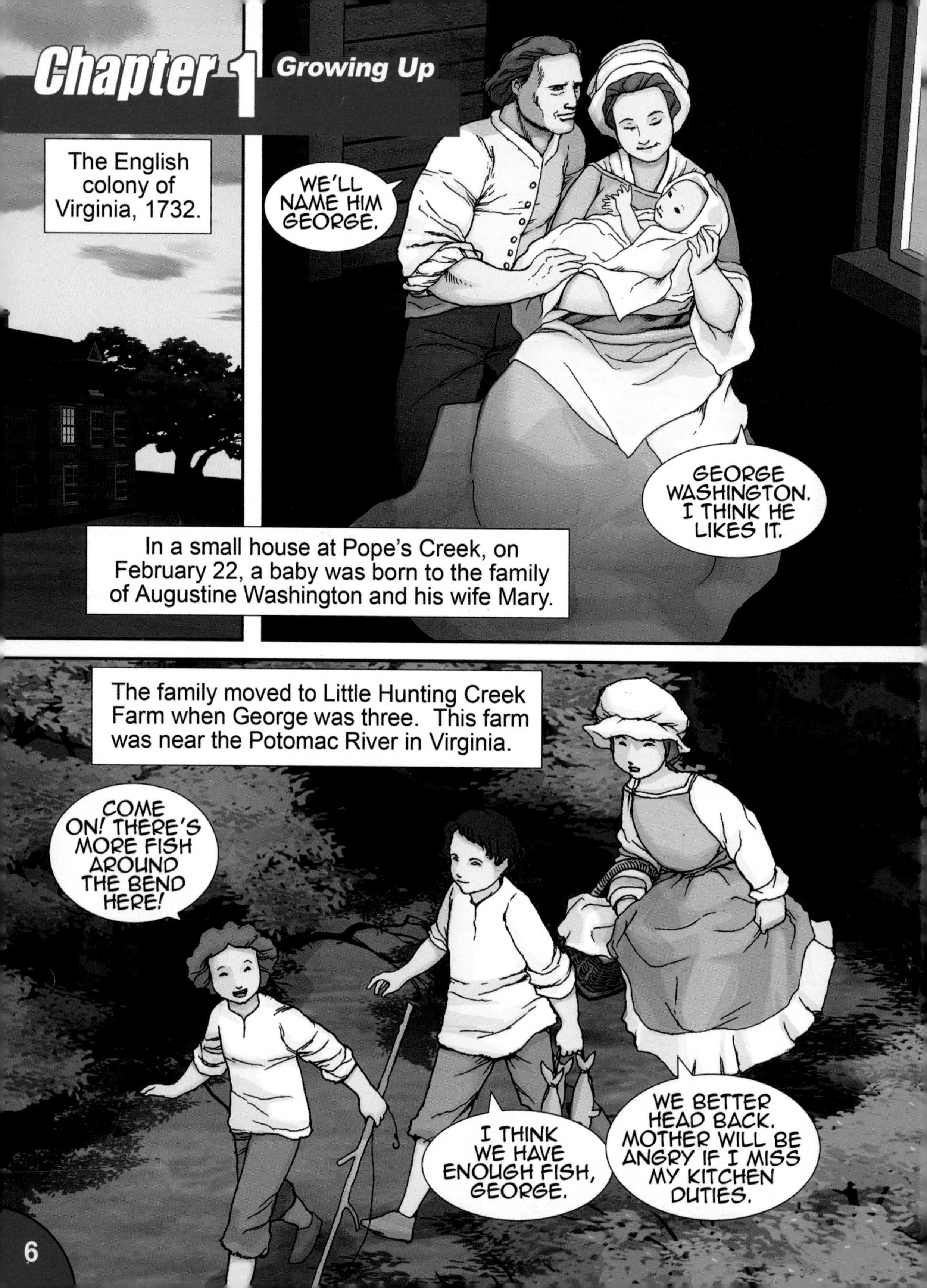
The English colony of Virginia, 1732.
WE'LL NAME HIM GEORGE.
GEORGE WASHINGTON. I THINK HE LIKES IT.
In a small house at Pope's Creek, on February 22, a baby was born to the family of Augustine Washington and his wife Mary.
The family moved to Little Hunting Creek Farm when George was three. This farm was near the Potomac River in Virginia.
COME ON! THERE'S MORE FISH AROUND THE BEND HERE!
I THINK WE HAVE ENOUGH FISH, GEORGE.
WE BETTER HEAD BACK. MOTHER WILL BE ANGRY IF I MISS MY KITCHEN DUTIES.

When George was 11, his father died. George had to leave school and help his mother with the farm.

George was close to his older half-brother Lawrence, who taught him hiking, riding horses, and arithmetic.

TELL ME WHERE THEY SENT YOU!

WE WERE SENT TO THE SPANISH STRONGHOLD OF CARTEGENA.

When he turned 16, George landed a job surveying land.

He liked this work because it combined his love of the outdoors with his love of mathematics.

Chapter 2 Army Career

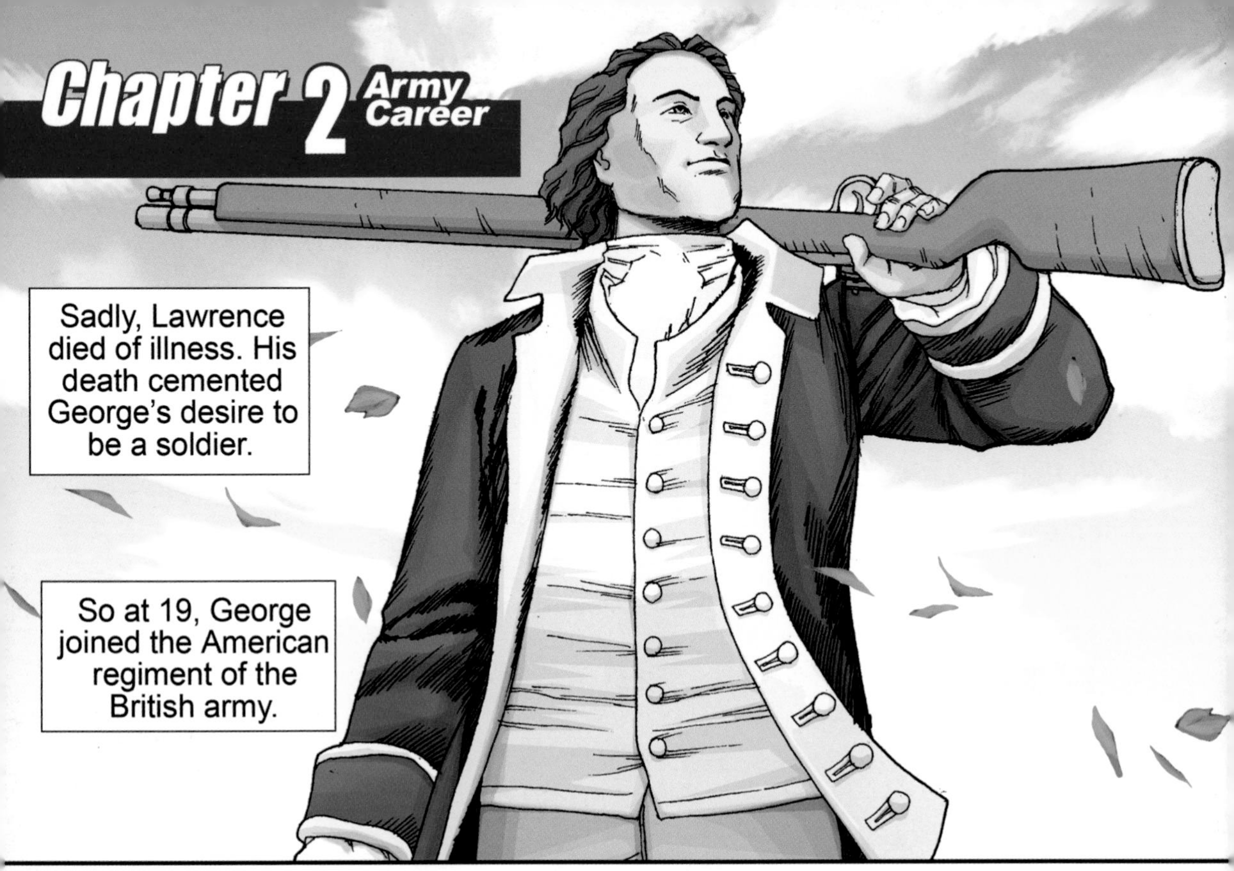
Sadly, Lawrence died of illness. His death cemented George's desire to be a soldier.
So at 19, George joined the American regiment of the British army.

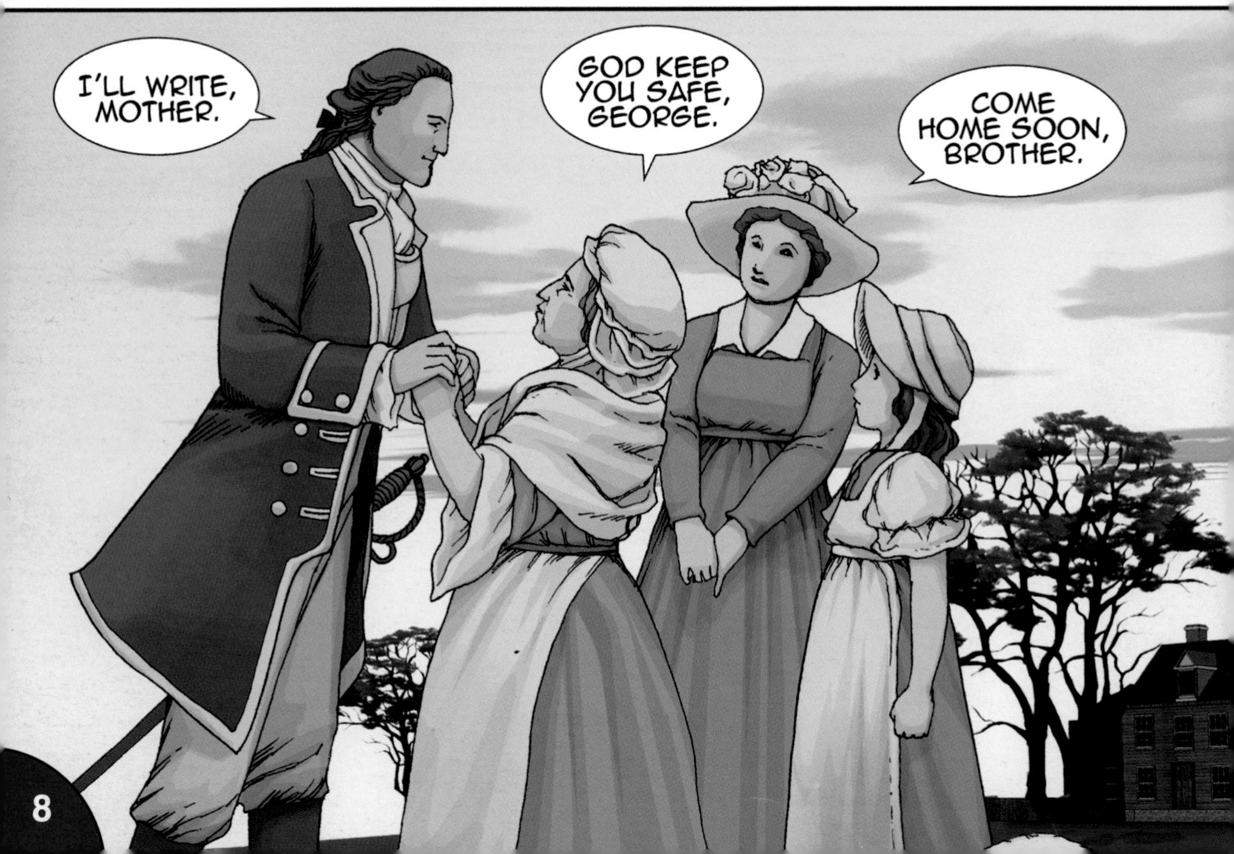
I'LL WRITE, MOTHER.
GOD KEEP YOU SAFE, GEORGE.
COME HOME SOON, BROTHER.

Washington was so good at soldiering that he was quickly promoted. He became a major in the colonial army at the early age of 20.

CHIEF HALF KING, WE CAN BUILD A FORT ON THAT RIDGE.

THE FRENCH HAVE BEEN SIGHTED THERE, MY FRIEND.

Washington was persuaded by Chief Half King to use the Indian strategy of surprise attack. This began a wider conflict that would spread halfway around the world.

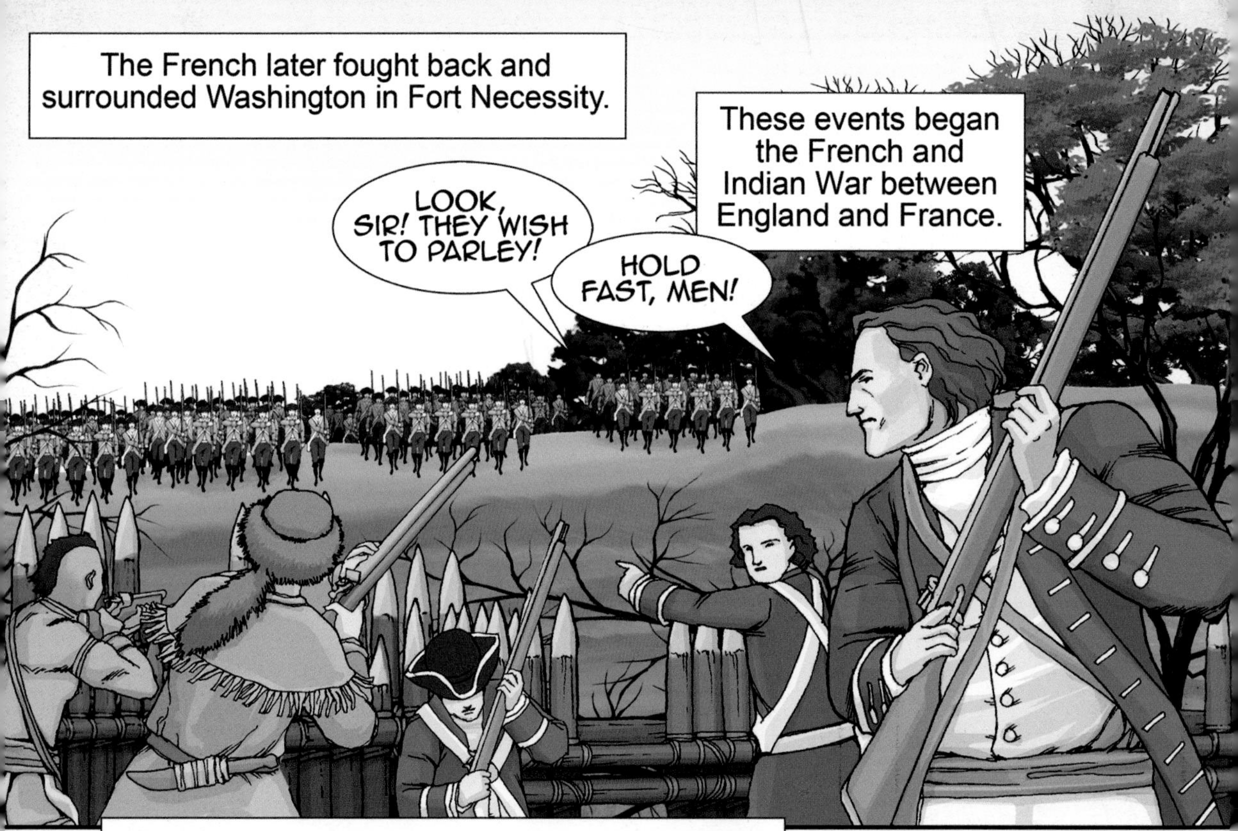
The French later fought back and surrounded Washington in Fort Necessity.
These events began the French and Indian War between England and France.
LOOK, SIR! THEY WISH TO PARLEY!
HOLD FAST, MEN!

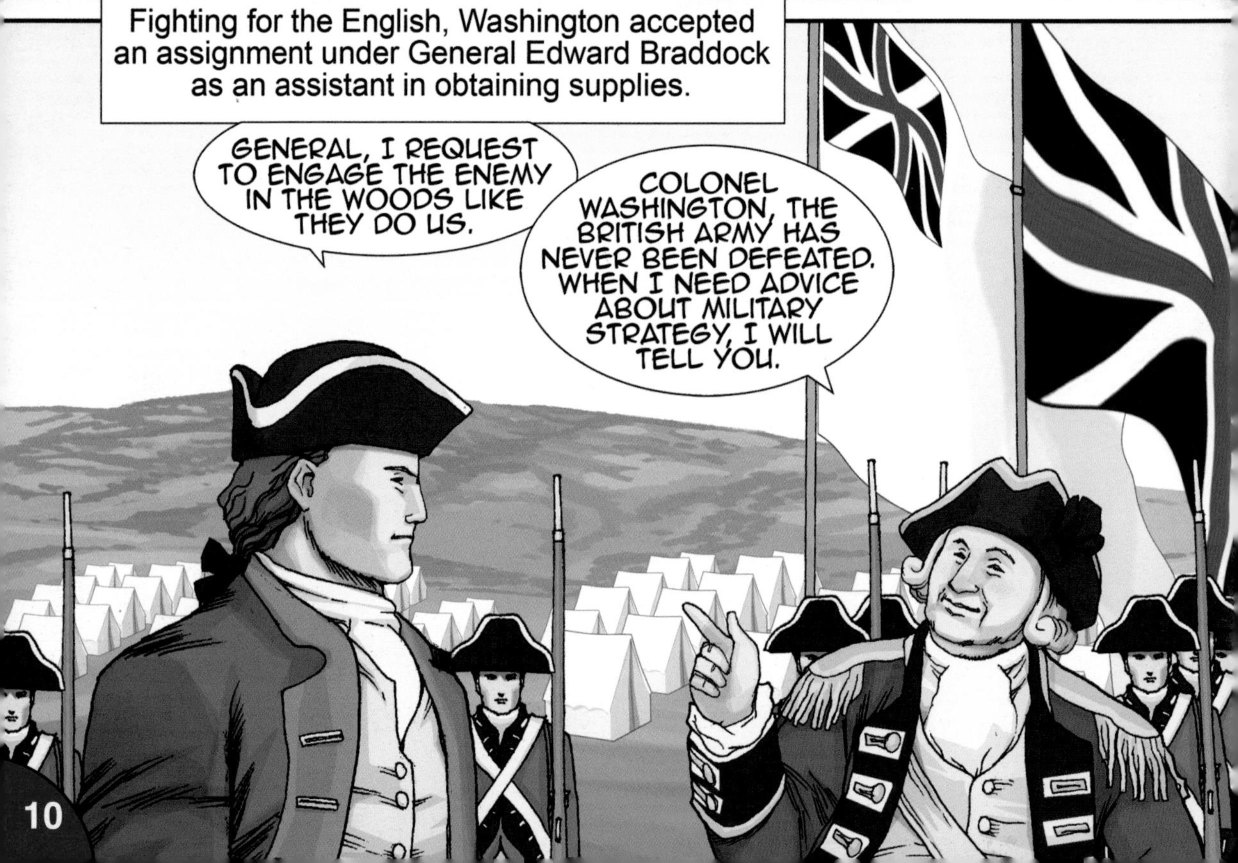
Fighting for the English, Washington accepted an assignment under General Edward Braddock as an assistant in obtaining supplies.
GENERAL, I REQUEST TO ENGAGE THE ENEMY IN THE WOODS LIKE THEY DO US.
COLONEL WASHINGTON, THE BRITISH ARMY HAS NEVER BEEN DEFEATED. WHEN I NEED ADVICE ABOUT MILITARY STRATEGY, I WILL TELL YOU.

The English army was used to fighting in the open and having many men in formation. The forested areas of North America were not good for these kinds of battles. The Native Americans and their French allies knew how to fight in the forests.

The British army's campaign was a disaster and the English retreated in disarray.

Washington had to carry his commanding officer off the field and march 40 miles back to the fort. Sometimes he had to crawl on his hands and knees to find the way.

KEEP FIRING!

The defeat later became Washington's victory. In Virginia, he became a hero for leading the survivors out of the ambush. His reputation grew throughout the colonies.

Washington went back to the site of his defeat. The French fled when they saw him coming. Washington found himself victorious without firing a single shot. He was active in the military from the age of 21 to 26.

The French and Indian War ended in 1758.

Chapter 3 — Family Life

In 1759, Washington went home to Virginia and married a widow named Martha Dandridge Custis.

For 16 years following his active war life, Washington was a private man.

Martha had two children from her first marriage. Washington cared for her son John Parke Custis called Jackie and her daughter Martha Parke Custis called Patsy.

THE LEES HAVE INVITED US TO A PARTY ON FRIDAY.

IT WILL BE GOOD TO SEE RICHARD AGAIN.

When he wasn't working, George and Martha attended many social events.

IT'S GOOD TO SEE YOU AGAIN, RICHARD.

LIKEWISE, GEORGE!

Washington was active in the Virginia Parliament. However, his business dealings with Europe and with England in particular left him unhappy.

GENTLEMEN, WE MUST DO SOMETHING ABOUT ENGLAND'S EXCESSIVE TAXATION OF OUR GOODS.

I AGREE. I CAN'T SELL MY TOBACCO WITHOUT ENGLAND MAKING ME A PAUPER.

Washington sold a lot of wheat and corn and soon had a mill of his own. He was a generous man. He allowed everyone to grind their wheat on his mill.

ONE DAY, I WILL NO LONGER NEED TO DEAL WITH ENGLAND. THEY BUY MY GOODS TOO CHEAPLY AND THEY SELL ME HIGH-PRICED EUROPEAN PRODUCTS.

Martha took care of the household. She cooked the family meals and she dried fruits from the plantation's many peach, cherry, and apple trees. She was very good at taking care of the house.

MAY I HAVE SOME PEACH JAM, MOTHER?

AFTER DINNER, PATSY.

The Washingtons were popular among their friends. They often had guests over for parties, dinners, and dancing.

COLONEL WASHINGTON! THIS IS A PLEASURE INDEED!

WELCOME TO MOUNT VERNON!

Washington lived a good life at Mount Vernon. But as the 1760s marched onward, the relationship between the colonies and England got worse.

WHAT IS IT, DEAR?

THE ENGLISH ARE INCREASING OUR TAXES AND TAKING AWAY OUR FREEDOM...

I HEARD. MANY PEOPLE ARE NOT HAPPY.

He knew the colonists could no longer live under British rule.

When the call came, Washington left Mount Vernon to work for his new country.

In 1774, Washington and other colonists met to decide what to do. They called themselves the First Continental Congress.

John Adams saw Washington at the meeting and decided he was still young enough to lead the continent into a new alliance.

YOU'RE A VETERAN OF THE FRENCH AND INDIAN WARS. GENTLEMEN, I VOTE TO ASSIGN COLONEL WASHINGTON TO LEAD US.

I SECOND THAT. YOU CAN LEAD THE CONTINENTAL ARMY!

Washington was voted the first commander in chief. This made him the leader of the armed resistance against the British.

He knew the assignment was beyond his experience. Although he knew they all faced a tough battle, he accepted the post.

Chapter 4 The American Revolution

On July 4, 1776, in Philadelphia, the First Continental Congress signed a paper called the Declaration of Independence. The battle for American independence had begun!

During the night, Washington had his soldiers build a fort on Dorchester Neck. The English were informed of the activity, but figured it could wait until morning.

The English were alarmed when they saw the fort that had sprung up overnight in front of them.

As fate would have it, a storm prevented the English from attacking.

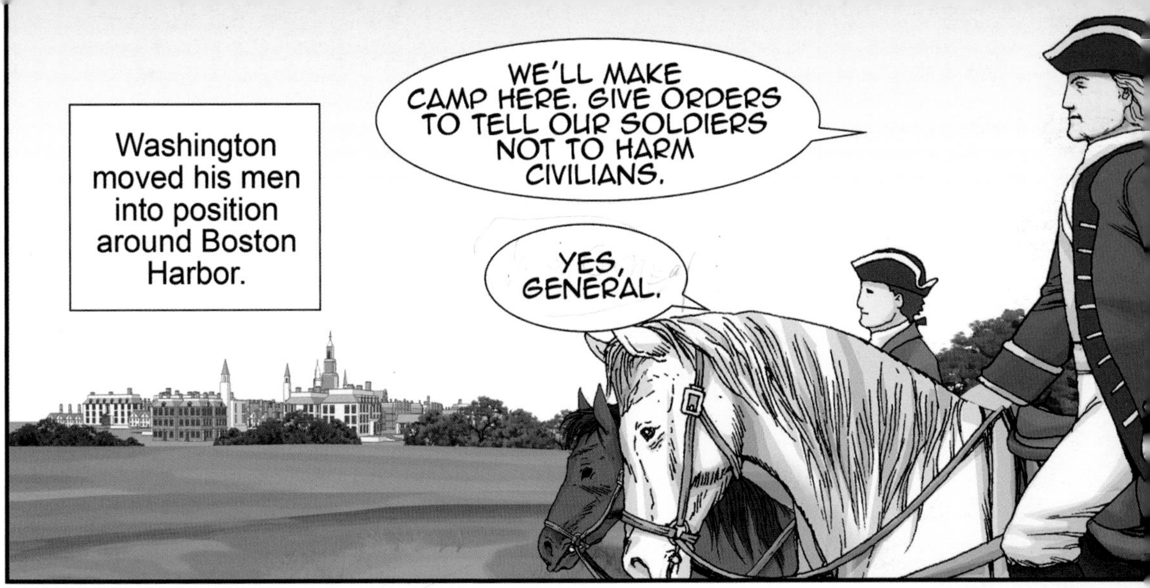
Washington moved his men into position around Boston Harbor.
WE'LL MAKE CAMP HERE. GIVE ORDERS TO TELL OUR SOLDIERS NOT TO HARM CIVILIANS.
YES, GENERAL.

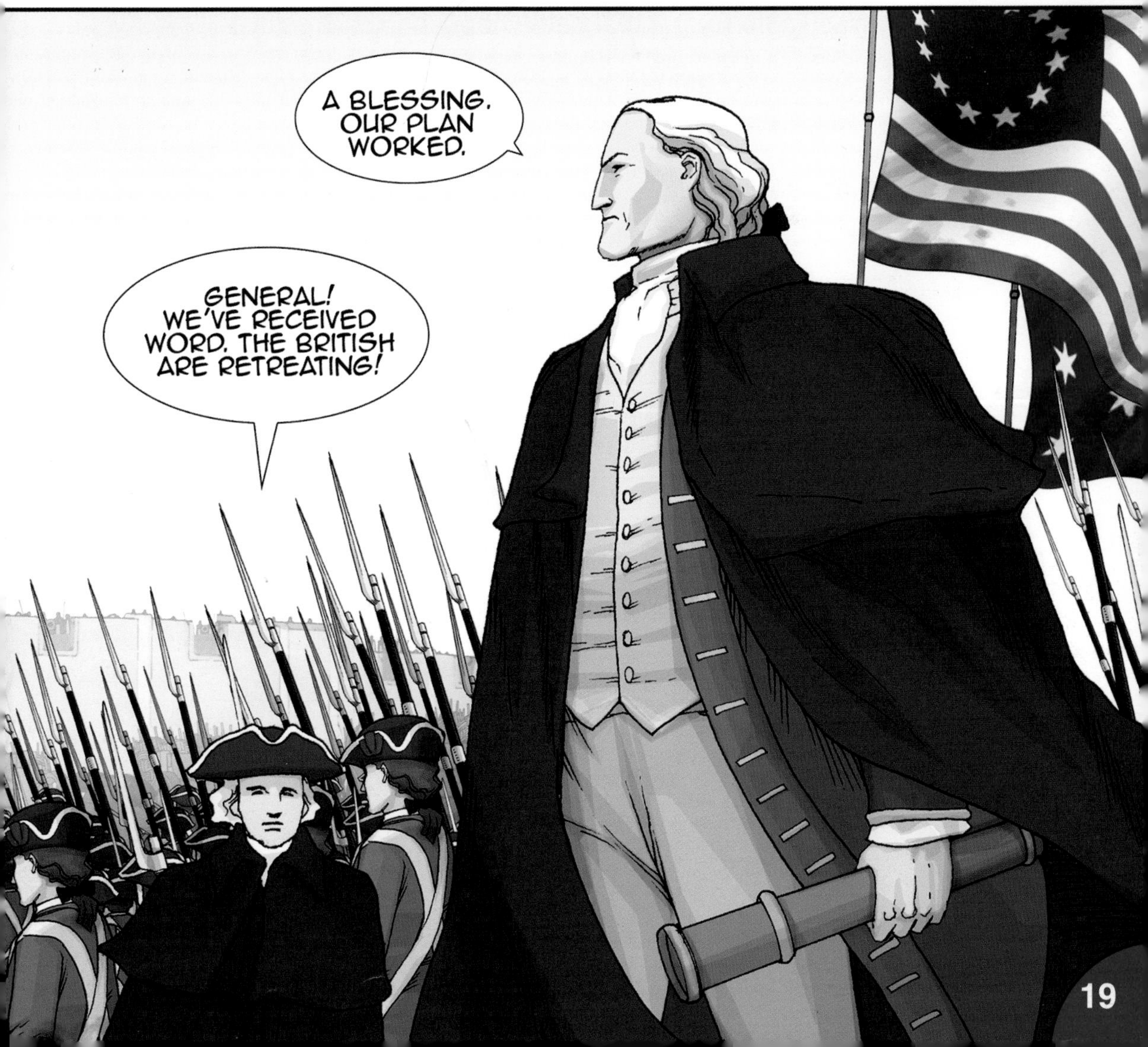
GENERAL! WE'VE RECEIVED WORD. THE BRITISH ARE RETREATING!
A BLESSING. OUR PLAN WORKED.

Washington's first real battle happened in Brooklyn Heights, New York, in 1776. The English brought soldiers from Germany to help them fight the colonists.

Although the American army was brave, it was made up mostly of farmers, bakers, and other volunteers.

Washington lost battle after battle. He lost many men to the British.

Against the British army, Washington's soldiers ran away!

STAND YOUR GROUND!

HAVE I GOT SUCH TROOPS AS THESE? ARE THESE THE MEN WITH WHOM I AM TO DEFEND AMERICA?

AAH!

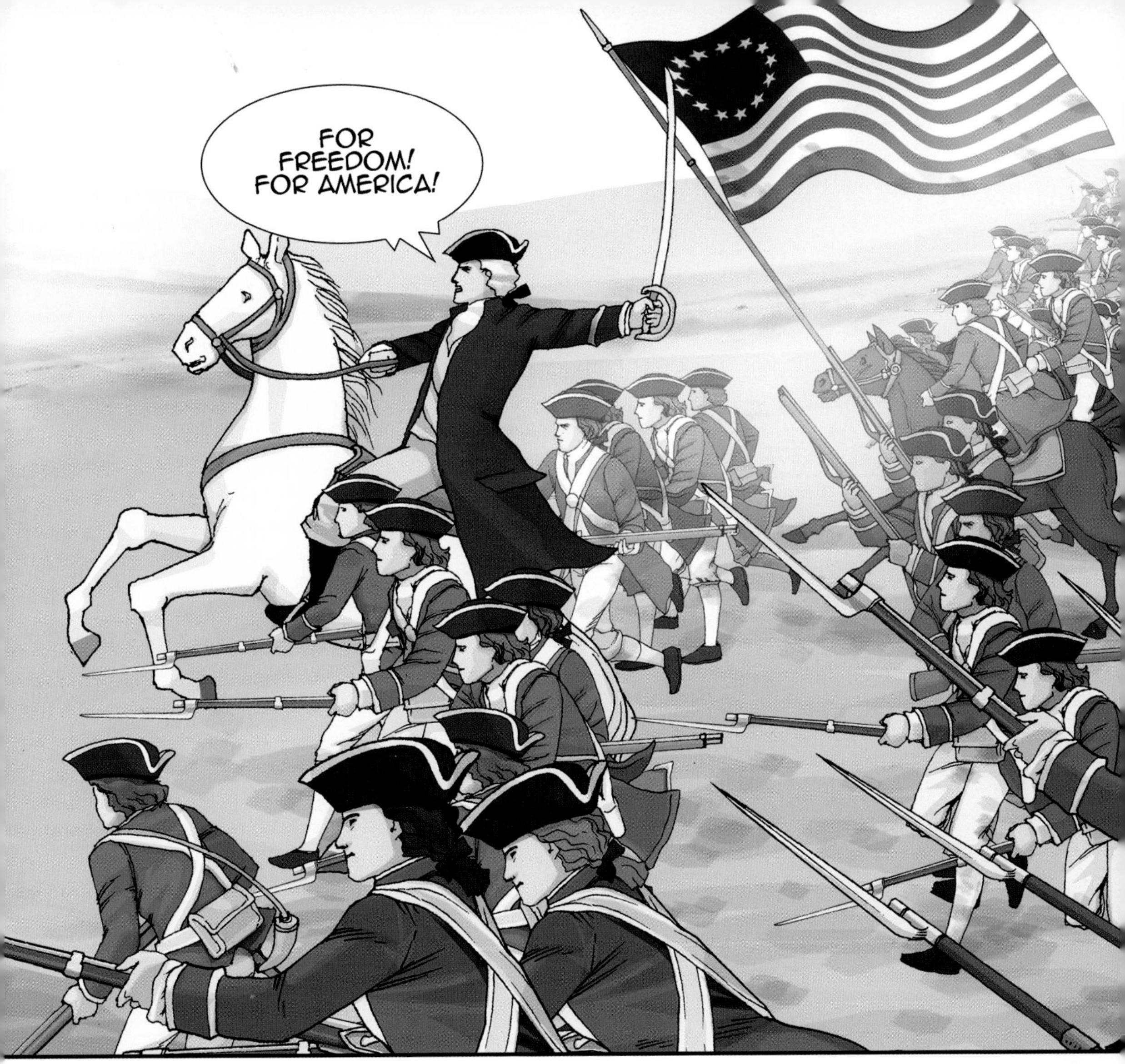
FOR FREEDOM! FOR AMERICA!

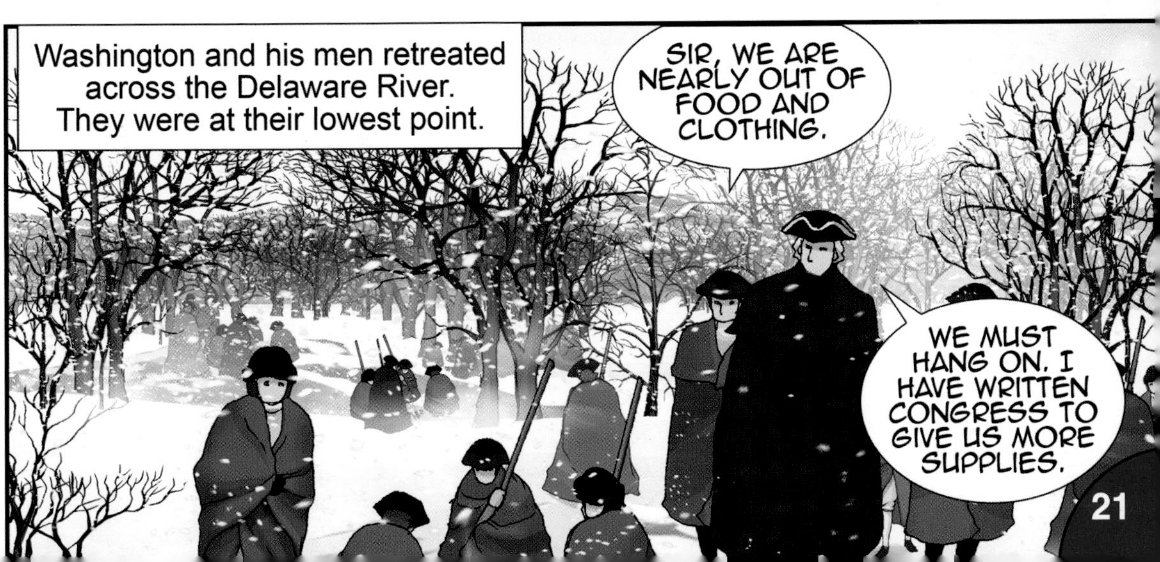
Washington and his men retreated across the Delaware River. They were at their lowest point.
SIR, WE ARE NEARLY OUT OF FOOD AND CLOTHING.
WE MUST HANG ON. I HAVE WRITTEN CONGRESS TO GIVE US MORE SUPPLIES.

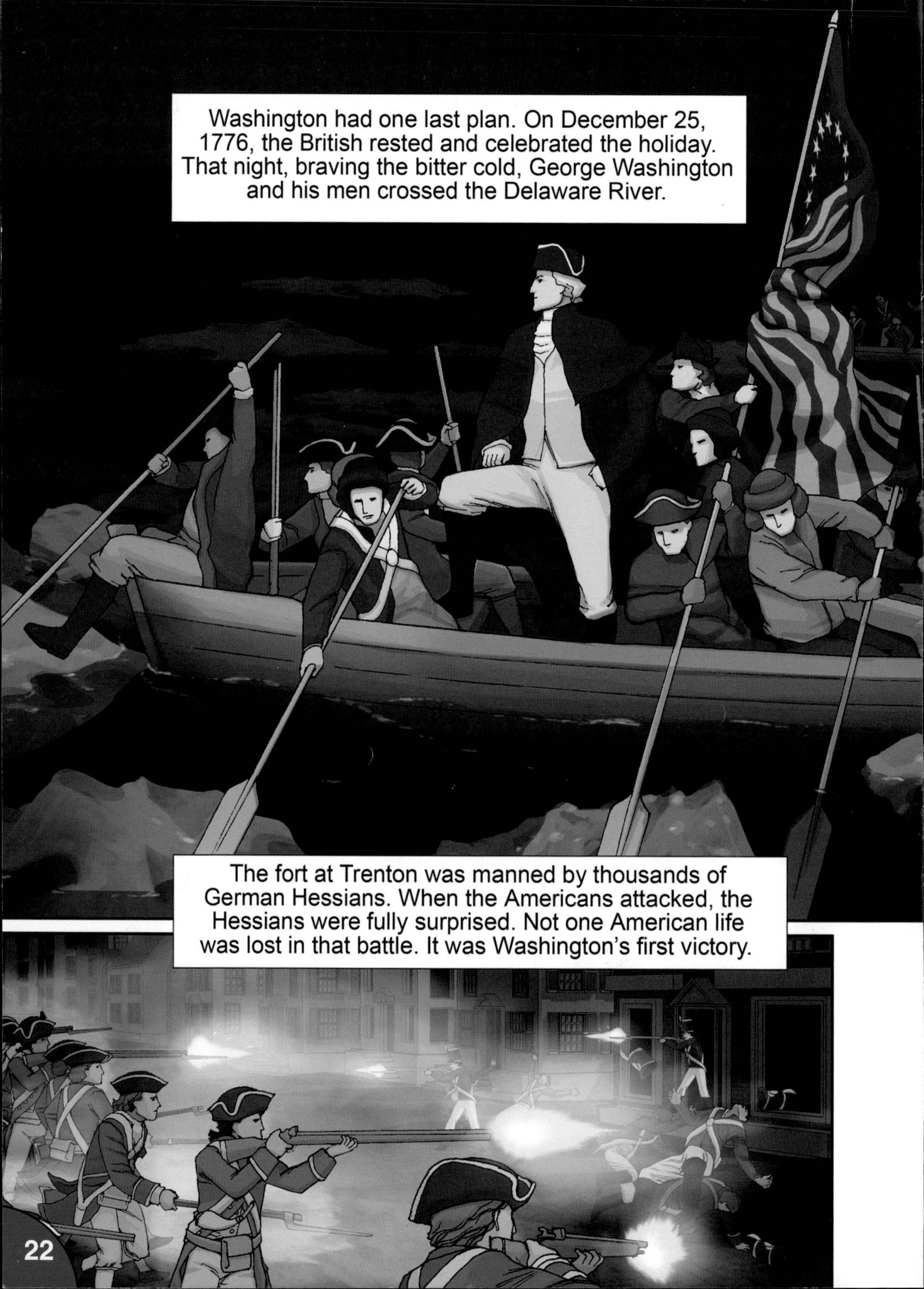
Washington had one last plan. On December 25, 1776, the British rested and celebrated the holiday. That night, braving the bitter cold, George Washington and his men crossed the Delaware River.
The fort at Trenton was manned by thousands of German Hessians. When the Americans attacked, the Hessians were fully surprised. Not one American life was lost in that battle. It was Washington's first victory.

They marched through many miles of cold and snow to the enemy's camp.

The war went on for many more years. The French got involved, aiding America against the British.

WELCOME TO MY CAMP, GENERAL ROCHAMBEAU.

DR. FRANKLIN SPEAKS HIGHLY OF YOU.

23

In 1780, French soldiers came to help the Americans fight a battle at Yorktown against Britain's Lord Cornwallis. Washington himself fired the first cannon, signalling the start of the battle.

CORNWALLIS CANNOT RETREAT BY SEA. THE FRENCH HAVE CLOSED THE BAY.

When Lord Cornwallis surrendered Yorktown in 1781, the colonists won the American Revolution. There were calls to make Washington king of America. But he refused.

THREE CHEERS FOR GENERAL WASHINGTON!

AMERICA IS NOW FREE FROM THE TYRANNY OF KINGS!

In 1783, Washington went home to Mount Vernon where he spent many years with his wife Martha in happy peace. He was 51 years old.

AT LAST... I AM HOME ONCE AGAIN.

THANK GOD YOU'RE BACK.

Washington traveled often and always tried new ways of farming his plantation. He enjoyed being home again. But the United States of America had new problems. The laws were not strong enough.

In 1787, Congress wrote a new Constitution. The Constitution described what the United States stood for and listed new laws. George Washington was elected the first president of the United States.

I FEEL I AM NOT UP TO THIS TASK, BUT I THANK YOU, GENTLEMEN, FOR YOUR CONFIDENCE.

He was inaugurated on April 30, 1789.

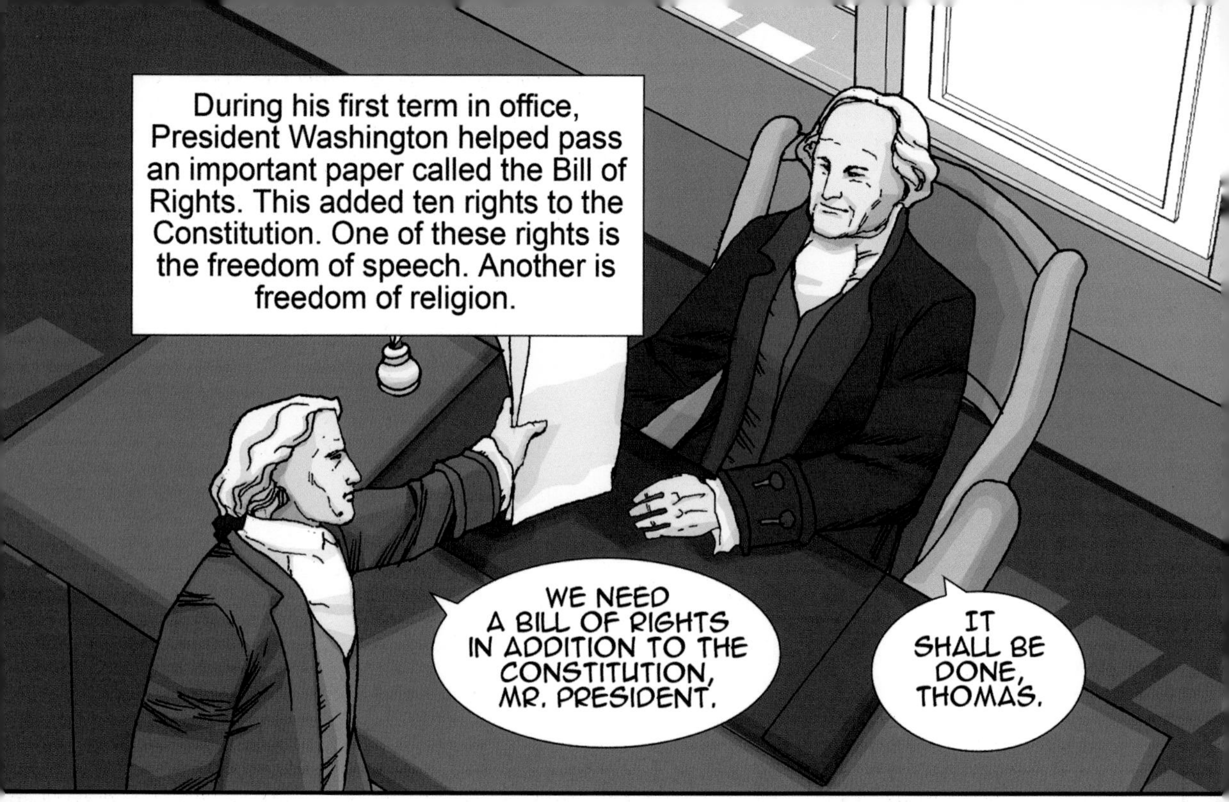
During his first term in office, President Washington helped pass an important paper called the Bill of Rights. This added ten rights to the Constitution. One of these rights is the freedom of speech. Another is freedom of religion.
WE NEED A BILL OF RIGHTS IN ADDITION TO THE CONSTITUTION, MR. PRESIDENT.
IT SHALL BE DONE, THOMAS.

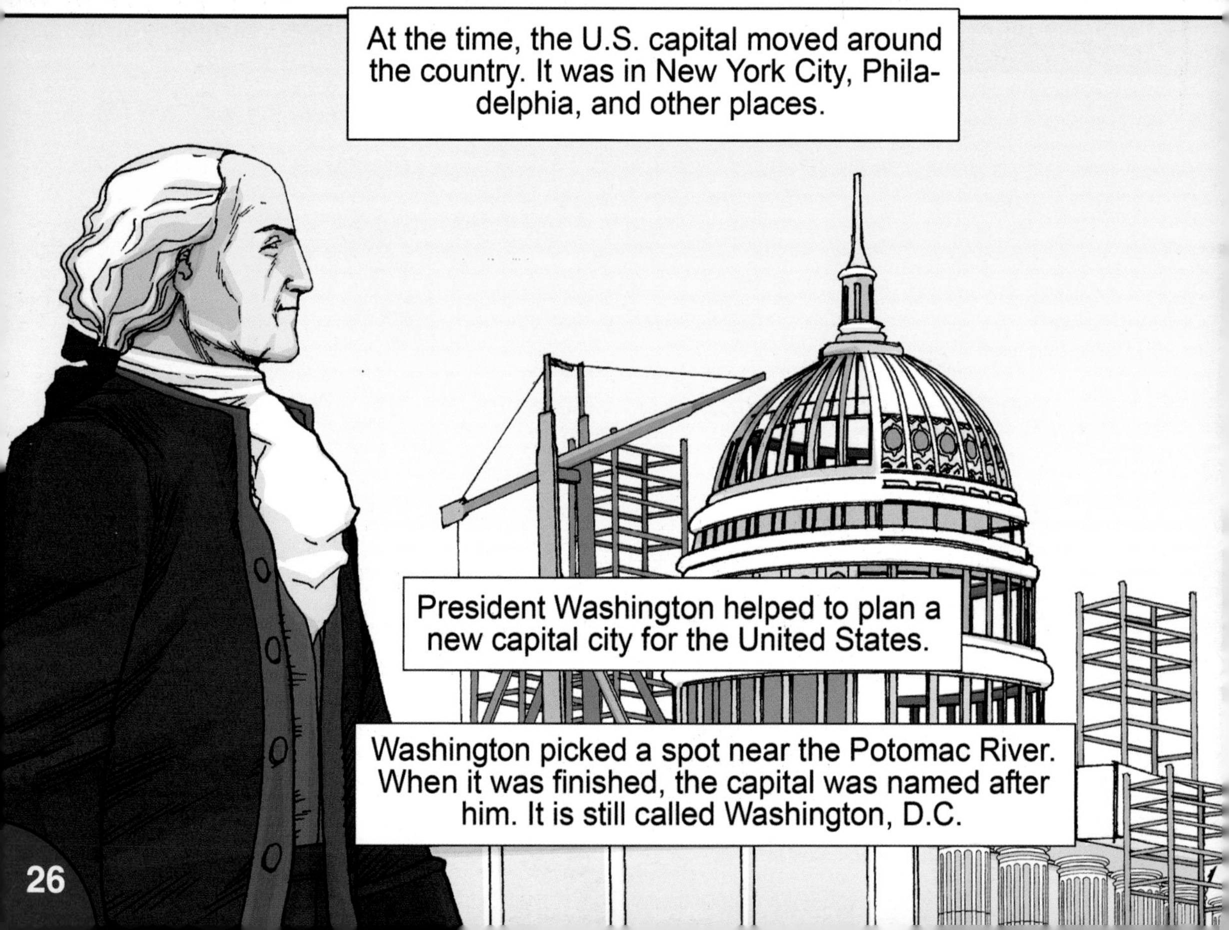
At the time, the U.S. capital moved around the country. It was in New York City, Philadelphia, and other places.
President Washington helped to plan a new capital city for the United States.
Washington picked a spot near the Potomac River. When it was finished, the capital was named after him. It is still called Washington, D.C.

Washington always remembered his days as a soldier during the French and Indian War. He later worked on behalf of the Native Americans. Washington worked hard to institute reforms on how they were treated. His reforms had a difficult time becoming law.

He formed new groups in the government called departments. As president, Washington picked the people to head these departments. They were called the cabinet. These departments are still part of the U.S. government today.

In 1792, despite his desire to retire from public service, Washington was elected to a second term.

THANK YOU FOR AGREEING TO SERVE AGAIN, GEORGE!

THANK YOU FOR YOUR CONFIDENCE, GENTLEMEN.

During his second term, Washington steered his country clear of the wars in Europe despite being asked to help out by France. He knew his country was not prepared yet to aid another country in a foreign war. He concentrated on building the industry and welfare of the people of the United States.

Washington retired in 1796 and returned home to Mount Vernon. He adopted two of Martha's grandchildren, Eleanor and George. The two children became part of the Washington household. Many people wanted Washington to run for a third term, but he would not hear of it.

IT'S GOOD TO BE HOME WITH YOU AGAIN, MARTHA.

DON'T LEAVE US AGAIN.

I WON'T.

George and Martha were busy those first few months entertaining guests.

In 1798, President John Adams asked Washington to help build a bigger U.S. Army.

I'LL SEE WHAT I CAN DO.

I NEED YOUR HELP, OLD FRIEND.

On a cold winter day, Washington rode his horse in heavy snow.

He got cold and wet and soon became very sick. On December 14, 1799, Washington died. He was 67.

People all over the world mourned his death.

To honor Washington's life and work for the country, a statue was proposed in 1783. Due to many problems, the plans were abandoned. A new memorial was begun in 1848 and completed 36 years later.

Today, visitors to Washington, D.C., can visit the Washington Monument and ride up to its observation deck.

Further Reading

Allen, Thomas B. *George Washington, Spymaster: How the Americans Outspied the British and Won the Revolutionary War.* Cambridge: Candlewick Press, 2007.

Gaff, Jackie. *George Washington: The Life of an American Patriot.* New York: Rosen Publishing Group, 2005.

Leighton, Marian. *George Washington.* Heroes of America. Edina: ABDO Publishing Company, 2005.

Welsbacher, Anne. *George Washington.* The United States Presidents. Edina: ABDO Publishing Company, 1999.

Glossary

allies - people or countries that agree to help each other in times of need.

ambush - a surprise attack from a hidden position.

civilian - a person who is not a member of the military.

inaugurate - to swear into a political office.

patriot - a person who loves his or her country.

tyranny - a government where one person has absolute power. The person in power is called a tyrant.

Web Sites

To learn more about George Washington, visit ABDO Publishing Company on the World Wide Web at **www.abdopublishing.com.** Web sites about Washington are featured on our Book Links page. These links are routinely monitored and updated to provide the most current information available.

Index